DAREDEVIL SPORTS

MOTOCROSS

By Peter Castellano

Gareth Stevens
PUBLISHING

HOT TOPICS

Please visit our website, www.garethstevens.com. For a free color catalog of all our high-quality books, call toll free 1-800-542-2595 or fax 1-877-542-2596.

Castellano, Peter.
Motocross / by Peter Castellano.
p. cm. — (Daredevil sports)
Includes index.
ISBN 978-1-4824-2984-8 (pbk.)
ISBN 978-1-4824-2987-9 (6 pack)
ISBN 978-1-4824-2985-5 (library binding)
1. Motocross — Juvenile literature. I. Castellano, Peter. II. Title.
GV1060.12 C378 2016
796.7'56—d23

First Edition

Published in 2016 by
Gareth Stevens Publishing
111 East 14th Street, Suite 349
New York, NY 10003

Copyright © 2016 Gareth Stevens Publishing

Designer: Samantha DeMartin
Editor: Kristen Rajczak

Photo credits: Cover, p. 1 taelove7/Shutterstock.com; p. 4 Maxim Petrichuk/ Shutterstock.com; p. 5 Ali Atmaca/Anadolu Agency/Getty Images; p. 7 PhotoStock10/Shutterstock.com; p. 9 Heritage Images/Hulton Archive/Getty Images; p. 11 Sherman/Hulton Archive/Getty Images; p. 13 moodboard/Cultura/ Getty Images; p. 15 Charles Imstepf/photolibrary/Getty Images; p. 17 John Thys/AFP/ Getty Images; p. 18 Igor Simanovskiy/Shutterstock.com; p. 19 anuphadit/ Shutterstock.com; p. 21 homydesign/Shutterstock.com; pp. 22, 26 Diego Barbieri/ Shutterstock.com; p. 23 John M. Heller/Getty Images Entertainment/Getty Images; p. 25 Teemu Tretjakov/Shutterstock.com; p. 27 Thananuwat Srirasant/Getty Images AsiaPac/Getty Images; p. 29 konmesa/Shutterstock.com.

Printed in the United States of America

CPSIA compliance information: Batch #CS15GS: For further information contact Gareth Stevens, New York, New York at 1-800-542-2595.

CONTENTS

EXTREME RACER

Imagine yourself speeding around a track made of dirt atop a lightweight motorcycle. There are hills to jump, corners to race around, and rocks and dirt flying everywhere. Would you be scared? Only a daredevil would try to race motocross!

RISK FACTOR

All motor sports are dangerous, and motocross riders are likely to get hurt. Only try a motor sport with the help of a knowledgeable adult.

Motocross is a kind of motorcycle racing that uses a lightweight motorcycle called a dirt bike. It takes place on a dirt track that riders have to **navigate** to try to be first over the finish line.

RISK FACTOR

Different kinds of motorcycle racing **events** may be on or off roads. Each kind uses a bike suited in size and speed for that event.

7

RACING HISTORY

Motorcycle racing started in the early 1900s. In 1924, a club in Great Britain planned an event in which the racers would speed around a dirt track, trying to finish first. They called it the "Southern Scott Scramble" and the sport "motorcycle scrambling."

RISK FACTOR

It's said that the event got its name because someone said,
"Whatever we call it, it will be a rare old scramble!"

Motorcycle scrambling soon became popular in France. The French called it "motocross," combining "motorcycle" and "cross-country." Interestingly, a similar sport began in the United States around the same time. However, the British were the best at motocross for many years.

RISK FACTOR

The first American to win
the world motocross championship
was Brad Lackey in 1982.

THE BIKE

Motocross bikes don't look much different from dirt bikes anyone can buy. The best motocross riders make their bikes lighter and more powerful. In races, they may go as fast as a car on a highway, depending on the track.

RISK FACTOR

There are two classes that race at a motocross event. They're divided based on engine size. Each class races twice.

RIDE WEAR

Motocross riders are taught to dress for a crash, not for a good ride. A well-fitting helmet is most important. Kneepads are often built in to motocross pants. Riders need boots covering their ankles, as well as goggles, gloves, and long-sleeve shirts.

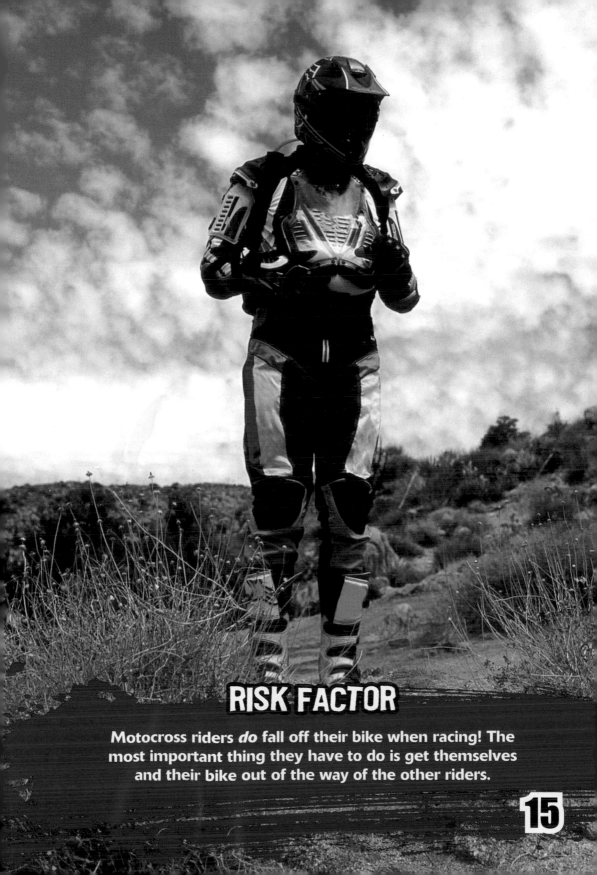

RISK FACTOR

Motocross riders *do* fall off their bike when racing! The most important thing they have to do is get themselves and their bike out of the way of the other riders.

READY TO RACE!

Today, there are **professional** and **amateur** motocross races. Pro races last 30 minutes plus two laps finished once the race leader reaches the finish line after that time. Amateur races may be based on a certain number of laps.

RISK FACTOR

Colored flags have different meanings during a motocross event.

start

caution; a rider is down or something is on the track

stop the race; there's a problem on the track

riders should move over to make way for the race leaders

one lap to go

the race is over

No motocross track is the same! They're 1 to 3 miles (1.5 to 5 km) long and have hills, dips, and turns at different places on each track. Riders have a chance to walk and ride on each track before they race.

RISK FACTOR

Motocross tracks are large enough so as many as
40 riders can race at a time.

The rules of a motocross event depend on its location. They may include bikes' speed on the track before races start. Rules often ban fighting and swearing. Riders who break rules may be **penalized** or even taken out of the race.

RISK FACTOR

Motocross riders are very fit! They use their body to control their bike. Some compare a motocross event to running very fast for 30 minutes!

MORE THAN MOTOCROSS

Supercross is a kind of motocross that takes place on a man-made course in an **arena**. There are lots of tight turns and high jumps, making the track an exciting ride! Speed is still important. Whoever finishes 20 laps first wins!

RISK FACTOR

Some pros, such as former racer Carey Hart, have raced in both motocross and supercross.

Imagine a motocross race that lasted 3 hours and took a rider through creeks, over rocks, and around forests. That's called enduro, short for "endurance," which means the ability to do something hard for a long time. Enduro racers are extreme!

RISK FACTOR

Motocross trials aren't races. Instead, motocross riders try to be the best at riding through **obstacles** like fallen trees without touching their feet to the ground.

Motocross daredevils can often do cool tricks on their bike. Freestyle motocross isn't about who's the fastest, but who can do the highest, biggest trick. Riders will jump over huge gaps or even spin their bike beneath them!

RISK FACTOR

The X Games are one of the biggest extreme sports events in the world. Taka Higashino won the gold medal in freestyle motocross in the 2013 X Games.

27

GETTING STARTED

Kids can start racing motocross at age 4—but you can start at any age! The first thing you need is a dirt bike and to learn to ride it. Once you're good at that, you can start picking up speed!

RISK FACTOR

Not interested in being a motocross rider yourself? Watching motocross races in person can be thrilling, too!

SAFETY TIPS

ALL MOTOCROSS RIDERS SHOULD:

- wear proper safety gear, including a helmet, kneepads, and boots.

- wear other proper clothing, including a long-sleeve shirt, gloves, and pants.

- take care in wet, windy, or icy conditions, as riding could be unsafe.

- check their bike before and after each ride for problems.

- take part in other exercise to remain fit enough to control their bike.

FOR MORE INFORMATION

BOOKS

Cain, Patrick G. *Moto X Best Trick.* Minneapolis, MN: Lerner Publications Co., 2014.

Monnig, Alex. *Motocross Racing.* Minneapolis, MN: ABDO Publishing Co., 2014.

WEBSITES

AMA Motocross Racing Photo Albums
www.motorcycle-usa.com/114/Motorcycle-Photo-Album/AMA-Motocross-Racing.aspx
Check out photographs of recent motocross races.

Transworld Motocross
motocross.transworld.net/
Read about motocross on the website of the biggest motocross magazine.

GLOSSARY

amateur: someone who does something without pay

arena: a place where a sporting event takes place

event: a happening

navigate: to find one's way

obstacle: something that blocks a path

penalize: to punish

professional: earning money from an activity that many people do for fun

INDEX